Home in the Stream

Home in the Stream

BY
Eleanor Limmer

RESOURCE *Publications* • Eugene, Oregon

HOME IN THE STREAM

Resource Publications
An Imprint of Wipf and Stock Publishers
199 W. 8th Ave., Suite 3
Eugene, OR 97401

www.wipfandstock.com

PAPERBACK ISBN: 978-1-6667-1027-4
HARDCOVER ISBN: 978-1-6667-1028-1
EBOOK ISBN: 978-1-6667-1029-8

For Leah, Alex and Aden Carl
Eric, Zachary and Maxwell Limmer
and Donald Limmer

Contents

Introduction

Home in the Stream describes in poetic form my spiritual quest for wholeness. This quest I feel is related to my destiny and my birth name "Holmstrom" in Swedish meaning home in a stream. I am a holistic counselor and poet who incorporates the messages of body, mind and spirit in my work as a poet and counselor. My parents were Swedish immigrants who owned a small grocery store in Seattle. I grew up spending much time in the forests around Seattle and the Puget Sound where I developed a love of nature and the waters of the Northwest. I lived in Alaska for four years. Since 1980, I am at home on the shores of Liberty Lake, near Spokane Washington

These poems were inspired by people or experiences in which I was deeply moved to express a profound sense of truth or beauty. When I express this inspiration in art or poetry, I become more complete or whole. I become more united with my highest spiritual self. In the poem, "Getting out of My Way," I describe how when I relax and go inward I can hear a voice which connects me to nature, spirit and others.

Home to me is more than a place, it is a consciousness of truth, love and peace. Going Home for me is a continual process, not just an inner or outer destination. This process means being awake to beauty in the present moment, but also having faith and courage knowing I am not alone and am part of the creative energy streaming through all of life. Writing these poems helped me transcend negativity in myself and grow into an awareness of being more complete and self-realized. These poems are a gift from the creative stream of life within me to help me and others to find our way back home.

The Forest Lover

for Emily Carr

The wild birds of her imagination
sang over her head, never enough paint
or words to capture them, her ideas as slippery
as kelp just off shore from a deep cedar forest.

It was the green force of spirit moving through space
she sought to capture in her art, the verdant ecstasy
and peaceful silence she felt in the deep forest places
where sky married shore, and the great red cedars
spoke to her of nature spirits and mystical beings
The natives of the villages she visited
called her "Klee Wyck" laughing woman
and noticed her casual, good humor and
courageous determination to sketch their totems.

She found the spiritual force within
these cedar monuments so compelling
she was willing to face swarms of mosquitoes
to reach the abandoned Native villages
then forsaken, dank, dilapidated and rank
with rotten wood and stinging nettles.

She longed to capture the maternal strength
she sensed in the great wooden hands
of the totem mother of Kitwancool that held a child,
with the tender strength of all womanhood
as if it grew at the heart of a giant red cedar tree

waiting for the native carver to chip away its outer wood
so the face of the great mother could be revealed.

She was inspired by the stark and sacred forests
of the Pacific North, the green cathedrals
and lush corridors of shadows leading into inner
chambers of light. The rhythmic patterns
she could only hear and see with her inner senses.
With her inner ears she heard the screams
of orphaned trees abandoned in clear-cut forests
after the loggers had left. She sensed the green
force that surrounded these spindly stragglers
the union of sky and trees
she had to close her eyes to see.

Good Fences

A border of day lilies
is all that separates us
from our friendly neighbors.
It is enough for us,
as for them. Only riotous dogs
or unruly children have violated
the sanctity of this secure delineation.

Every day in July the day lilies
trumpet out their profusion,
each one centered in bright yellow,
wild tongued and gorgeous
as a tiger's mane
blasting out daily tributes
to the sun in exuberant shades
of burnt sienna and orange.

Each day lily makes a brief
singular statement, unique
and bold, yet part
of a lavish display.

This abundant border
resonates the subtle statement:
"Life is open and abundant here.
You can walk along this path
without being threatened.
You are safe to be yourself,
yet open to the world."

Sunset on the Sound

and the last of the flotilla of fishing boats
chug their way into port, heavy laden
with escapee fish, undesirable invaders
who fled their crumpled netted cages
and slipped into foreign waters.

Atlantic fish in Pacific waters
an invasive species
violators of the natural order
on the wrong side of the sea
dangerous threats to the survival
of Orca whales, young wild salmon
and the Marbled Murrelet.

The clear waters of the Puget Sound
polluted by the ghosts
of unborn wild salmon
their human perpetrators blaming
the prisoner escape on mother nature
unprecedented high tides
and the fluke of an eclipse of the moon.

You can hardly blame the fish
for escaping confining metal pens
and joining their southern neighbors
in a wild, free dance.

This heroic mission to save endangered species
was no easy catch with its long days
harvesting only a small percentage
of the despised, displaced foreign fish.

Weaver Woman

I spin out into space upon the threads
and sensitive filaments of my intuition
trusting my dreams and strongest impulses
 to connect me to the ultimate weaver,
the one with infinite patience
who begins again each new moment
using the threads I choose to give her
to weave the poetry of my soul.

The weaver woman accepts whatever
threads or fabrics I give her
respecting the directions
of my passionate desires and dreams
either a transcendence of the past
with joyful fulfillment and achievement
or the prison of a web of suffering and pain.
the destruction the black dog of my fears.

Even when I fall asleep or let the black dog
destroy my best threads or fabrics,
she is still there listening with intent
for my finest moments, my most brilliant
breakthroughs of thought and feeling
my most luminous and innovative ideas.

She knows under the chaos and confusion
a new form is emerging within me,
 every new day she forgives
 and begins to weave again
using the warp of my vibrant ideas
and the woof of my dream of freedom
weaving the tapestry of my new life.

The Shadow Knows

what we hate most
about our intimate others
the hostile punishments
and cruel judgments
we refuse to face in ourselves

the charlatan's truth
collected and held
until he cares enough
to be honest, the servant's courage
held until she is strong enough
to stand up to her oppressor

the hungry dogs of our passions
we did not feed
that haunt us in our dreams
and bite us with a speeding ticket
or a serious disease
when we neglect to nurture
our most precious self

in the basket of our soul the shadow
holds the dark mirror of anger or fear
blinding us to the goodness
in the face of the strangers

as a champion of our truest self
the shadow collects and holds
essential pieces of ourselves
the light or talent we inhibit or discard
until we are wise or strong enough
to claim it as our own

The Ear in the Sky

Even though we are only tourists traveling through
our young Navajo guide shares with us
her reverence for the monuments of stone
of her Native land. With a vulnerable authority,
she shows us the places,
sacred to her and her ancestors.

Under her wide brimmed felt hat,
her long black hair glistens in the sun.
As comfortable behind the wheel of a truck
as she is out in the red sands of her reservation,
she tells us about her medicine man grandfather,
and her desire to follow his heritage of healing.

She takes us to a place called the Ear of the Sky
 a sacred portal of sound. A round hole
in an arch of red stone high above our heads
open to the deep blue sky.
With the beat of her drum
our guide invites us to listen to the spirits
within and around this powerful place.

We are quiet listening for guidance
the pulse of the earth, directions of where to go,
the beat of our hearts telling us
who we could love and hold dear
the call of those to whom we belong.

This hole moans for all who suffer
alone and abandoned,
hollow of hope and vision.
It hears the suffering of the Navajos
those oppressed and imprisoned
who refuse to beat open their dreams.

The ear of the sky listens
for signs of green hope in the dry desert
the heart beats of new life
growing out of the red sands
of our deepest longings.

In Muir Woods

As we enter the woods,
a pungent freshness enfolds us
with an unusual intimacy
seldom found in a public park open
to visitors from all over the world.

a quiet stream meanders
down the middle of the woods
we cross wooden bridges
surrounded by boardwalks
accessible to wheelchairs.

We admire the fire-scarred redwoods
survivors of firestorms, some burnt to their core
in her wheelchair, my friend Carole
is a survivor too from cancer and chemo-therapies
toppling her to the ground.

Her son playfully maneuvers her wheelchair
into the black cave under a burned-out redwoods
so she can feel its strength and connect
with the life in its tranquil healing center.

He pushes her close enough to a redwood
so she can stroke its thick rough bark close enough
 to hug the huge trunk of the giant tree.
Later she tells me, "Our trip to Muir Woods
was the first time since I moved to California,
I felt completely at home."

Freedom

I can choose to remain on the shore
safe and stagnate, or to pour myself
into the blue current of adventure
where I am as likely to find beautiful
boulders as a china pheasant.

Safety is the price I pay
for the thrill of the rapids,
being true to my inner compass,
the challenge to rebel against
the rulers of society who punish
the knuckles of my dignity.

The current of the river breaks open
the shoals of my pain and exposes
the majestic cartography that awaits
and strengthens me at every bend.

Free to wander the purple fields
of my imagination, I can float
or swim at my own pace, conscious
of the responsibilities of my conscience,
but free of compulsions, duties
or obligations that are not mine.

I listen to the music the river
makes as it flows over the rocks
and see the sparkle of my face
reflected in the whirlpools.

I give myself permission
to surrender my sense of separation
to feel what has been granted-
the flow of the river in my veins,
the strength of the current
carrying me toward the sea.

Daring to Fly

The year begins with a shift in the polar vortex
allowing us to feel Arctic air,
the extremes of cold and warmth
the paradox of climate change.

When the sun warms
the tight lid of the ice over the lake,
depth charges drum out reverberations
ruminations of sounds
the beat of ancient battles.

Drunk on mountain ash berries,
a waxwing crashes with a thud
against our window pane,
its proud plume and embellished feathers
flickering between life and death,
stunned and quivering on the frozen ground.

I too have been knocked down
by glass windows I did not see,
the arctic air of failures or falls
which left me stunned or frozen
yearning for wild flight.

With the waxwing, I disgorge
the bitter fruit of frustration
and awaken to new, better ways
to be free, lifting out
of the spell of fatal endings,

the old reasons to despair or hide
from whatever barriers
I no longer need to fear.

The 11th Hour

for Ed Tyler 11/11/2011

Our cells chime out their connections
to the perceptions from our centers,
streaming out the secrets they hold
once hidden from us
in the most apparent places,
the twist of an arm, the ache of a heart,
the bend of a knee, clear as the nose
on our faces, no longer front page news
just information, messages we might
not wish to know, but now here.

A mirror we hold up to our faces
in which we could see our wrinkles
as ancient relics of a life well lived
or sunken ruins of judgment and despair.
It is all there in our perceptions,
how we view the cup we are given
Is it a precious gift, or not enough to satisfy?
Is it golden leaves of autumn,
or the grin of a skeleton's skull?

As we wonder where that woman
or man we used to be has gone,
we can look deeper into our faces,
and see in our old eyes at last
the face of wisdom smiling back at us,

with more compassion, kindness
and honesty than we have ever known,
finally accepting our timeless minds,
the grace of our eternity,
the purity of a wiser vision.

The Divorce

He could fix anything but not this foreign car
they drove with such competitive fury.
He had no heart to try to repair
what he felt was no longer his.

Their marriage became an unfortunate accident,
with shattered glass and engine parts
and frightened children cowering
beneath shards of anger and the remnants
of what was once an elegant car
now immobile and stagnant
in a field of bitterness and pain.

What was once vital and whole
now oozed oily debris and scattered parts
in a field once fertile and green.

Someone drove this vehicle too hard and fast
filling it with high octane gas
when it needed only regular fuel
oil changes and attention paid
to its vulnerabilities and weaknesses.

Small indiscretions and regrets
were followed by negligence
and a lack of attention to intimate parts
until a final act of infidelity drove
it around a sharp corner into a ditch.

It is too late now to restore it to its former grace,
or to find the foreign parts it needs to replace
those which no longer fit together
in any viable coherence.

Corroded by rust and storms,
its doors no longer open.
The promise of this elegant vehicle lost.
A family mourns knowing it is better,
to walk away than try to fix
what is beyond repair.

Connections

for Leah

My body was the bow
from which your arrow flew
the spaceship from which you hung
suspended upon a slender cord
how short a time, you lie cuddled
and hidden below my rib cage
imprinting yourself upon my heart
with a full, ripe savor.

After that first cord was cut
we built a rope between us strong enough
to hold two mountain climbers,
but as sensitive as exposed wires.

Now as you are propelled away
from me into space
I cut the rope between us and watch
you land upon your feet.

Your absence sometimes feels
like air knocked from my lungs
limp sails upon a windless sea.

The wind from which the boat
of your body breathes free
impels me toward my own port,
May the wind be full and warm

enough to fill the hollow
here below my heart

What connects us
is invisible fingers on the strings
The hands that hold the arrow
hold the bow
may its bending be for gladness.

To Preserve, Protect and Defend

After a bitter year of disease and division
we glimpse the blue sky beyond
if we are brave enough to imagine
the unity beyond separation
the peace beyond anger and fear.

If we care enough to remember
although democracy is fragile,
it is as strong as the light
within us, when we stand up
to the deception of a demagogue
then we will sense the unity
beyond our separations
the light beneath our darkest night.

When we are humble enough
to enter the sunlit room within us
where our higher self waits
to embrace us with the sun
of its wisdom, the compassion
of its eternal peace and grace.

Then we will be wise enough
to preserve, protect and defend
our heritage of freedom
to feel the warmth of the sun
upon our upturned faces
the bright joy of welcome
the peace of wholeness

we will know
when we find our way home.

Coming of Age

Although others tell you
it is all down hill from here,
you can look at this pinnacle in time
as a circle closing to eternity
where you can see the vast sky beyond
cushioning and supporting your steps,
the wisdom of a broader point of view.

You can allow yourself to craft your adventure,
seeing each person you meet
as singular as an avalanche lily,
giving yourself permission
to be your own horse and rider,
letting no one else control your reins.

No longer waiting for someone
to approve of your strengths,
you can enter the narrows
and glimpse the light that pours
toward you from the other side.

In this light is your true face,
the one you choose to wear
before you were born, when
you are strong, and wise enough
to surrender to your own road.

Beloved

for Don

Something told me
when you first held my hand,
you would never let go
there was safety in your touch,
fertile ground I could depend upon
to be firm, for us to grow together.

Partners since our youth,
we each keep growing
bolstered by the others' support
and good intent, each of us
as unique as a Redwood or a Douglas Fir
buffering each other from sickness and storms
strong enough together
to build a home to last a century.

Your large hands have grown
calloused and hard
yet more tender, open
and generous with the years.

Always dependable, there is nothing
I need of you, you would deny.
Guardian of the waters, you keep watch
so storms do not carry away our earth.

Whenever I ask for more freedom, you say, "fly."
You are the first to push me off the ledge
of my fear. You open the door for me wide,
knowing, I will always return
to be near your side.

Storm Water Run-off

Somewhere high up it all started
to trickle down and come apart
at the seams of what matters,
long before the Spring storms
split open the skin of the earth
and the hillside slide and spoiled the lake,
roots were pulled up, the connections
to what is elemental severed,
trees upon the green slopes
mowed down like grass
and golden fields of feeling armored
by parking lots and housing projects.

Just when we think it does not matter
what happens, then the storms spew
their sludge into our streams
and the pain of the deep mind-cuts flood
the pure lake of our consciousness with mud.

After the wetlands are capped by concrete
the storm water has no place to seep
there is no sump to breath in or out
no place to absorb the waters of emotion
but into the mouth of the lake
so vulnerable and deep
that the sludge of a careless word,
a thoughtless deed
kills the fingerlings of what is alive in us,
and chokes the streams to the spawning ground
somewhere higher up where it all started.

The Blessings of Living Near a Lake

That it reflects a sense of fullness
where one can be entranced
for an afternoon, or a life time,
every moment changing
one moment smooth and serene,
the next pulsating
with deep unheard sound.

A clearing in the confusion,
a watery meadow
to graze and feel suspended
in its shining surface.

In the evening, it melts
into a sunset of honey or magenta,
smooth to the taste
reflecting the lavender hills licked
by the last rays of the sun.

Today it is a plateau of peace
a feeling of home
where I breathe in a field of freshness
melted yellow, greens and blues
broken by an occasional
mallard, osprey, or merganser.

Ah, what generosity of space!
holding the farthest shore
and whatever is served
upon its outstretched and ample table.

Freeing Matisse's Birds

What would free the birds from the flat
wooden surface of my front door?
I chip away at the wood
listening to the messages the birds hold
looking deeper and deeper into the grain
for the words and forms
carrying the joy of healing,
the ecstatic dance of freedom.

As stolid as Michelangelo's Slaves
their static patterns
are ideal forms defying
whatever swallow's grace is buried
in the grains of wood,
mere suggestions and promises
of the potential of swallows
to swoop and soar
in the joy of Spring.

I sharpen the carving tools
of my imagination, passion and desire
to remove the oppression and dross
of laughing gulls silenced
ancient pelicans mired in oily malaise
the foul stink of insignificance.

My sea hawk eyes scan the wood
for what is beneath the surface
waiting to emerge, then cut beneath
layer after layer of indifference,
impatience, and greed, allowing the birds
to be what they are meant to be:
osprey plunging under the waves,
swallows spiraling between the trees,
flying into the exhilaration of the air.

Enchantment

The evening sun burnishes
the water in golden light
displaying an island
off to the left of imagination
suspended in obscurity
shrouded in veils of fog.

The glory of the moment
invites us to enter enchantment
an opportunity to sail into its current
to look deep and see in the distance,
something round and full
an island of mystery, the promise
of rich possibilities for fulfillment
something extraordinary
beyond the mundane shadows
of chaos and conformity.

There is a presence here
an avenue of hope to be trusted
a golden passage way
to sail out beyond the darkness
of the comfortable and mediocre
into the adventure just ahead,
the beautiful unknown life
or death of the mystery beyond.

Bushwhacking

When you are beaten
into the tracks of the common road,
it is time to be a stranger
and break your own trail
time to let your wild path rise
up to greet your wilderness.

Then eager for the first sight of home
you set out through the swamp grass
following the hound's ear of your intuition.

You let the clear stream of you inner senses
sniff out the way
the land flows to meet you
allowing your deer eyes.
and your coyote cunning
guide you around thickets
and over fallen logs.

Following your inner compass
you choose the gentle pine needle path
on the other side of suffering
on the other side of the common road's
impossible promise.

You seek the wild road
that is seeking you
the only one
that knows your way home.

Bleeding Hearts

Pink hearts strung on a vine
each one dripping a tear
of white compassion holding a seed
of hope in its center.

When the pink hearts fill with sun,
they split open and grow two wings.
ready to drop their seeds
and open to whatever tears
need to flow through them.

From what greater love
did these pink hearts spring?
Was it from the heart of Mother Mary,
Kwan Yin, Buddha or Christ Jesus
that these hearts sprung?

My heart splits open
and grows wings at the sight
of these exquisite messages of love.
It fills up with the sun
of the greater love
from which these hearts bleed.

Landlord of Death

When death comes to evict
me from the rented rooms of my body,
with his dust pan and broom
to sweep me into the ashes
of yesterday's fire, I will change my old,
tattered clothing and step
into the dark mansion of mystery.

I will leave behind
what I thought was home
what was only a temporary loan,
the broken bones of change
the nickels and dimes of dollars
that cannot measure the value
of what there is in me
that will never be lost.

Within all the little deaths and losses
I have known
I know the white rose that opens
in dreams and reveries
where I can not be lost,
am on solid ground,
an island in a turbulent sea,
an elixir of the eternal
containing all the love
I have given or received.

Nests

Cups of creation, wombs of imagination,
each one a monument to mystery,
and the patience and perseverance
needed for any creation to fly free.

Last summer, a robin built a nest
in the plum tree outside our front door.
She crafted it with mud and twigs,
and tended it with devotion
through the hot summer days,
until her eggs hatched,
the hungry mouths were fed,
and the needy chicks finally flew free.

This empty nest and others now sit
upon ledges on my fireplace.
Each nest an archetypal form,
a majestic reminder to nurture
and mold my thoughts and feelings
with commitment, conviction and courage.

These nests remind me to honor
anyone or thing willing to mother
a new thought, child, feeling, or bird
into a world too busy to admire
what is free and wet with wonder.

Healing my Inner Child

To hold you against the cold night of your fear,
protecting you from your feelings of abandonment
child of my morning
innocent eyed and open
for something that was lost somewhere in time
the father who was sucked into the white sheets of death
the mother lost among the vegetable bins of her grocery store.

Your caretaker, Mamma Ahl had cement stairs
always too hard and difficult for you to climb
her house smelled of stale potato chips and oil
She did her best to save you from the sins
you never knew you were guilty of having.

I recall dandelion chains and a stage of lawn
in which you and your playmates produced
great dramas of make believe
dressed up in high heels, hats and adulthood.

I give you the love and attention you lost
and take back your creativity and wonder
the searching head always thrust forward
the eager arms open
to grasp a butterfly to love and be loved.

Be free, so we can face this world together
as adventure and going home.

Viking Son

for Eric

Hair of wild wheat
the smell of new mowed hay
curling wantonly
around a cherub's face.

Dionysus in disguise
behind his impish grin
there lies the brashness
of generations of vikings
poised to leap
upon my tired back.

Even in my womb
you were a restless one turning
yourself over at my request.
There was always gentleness
beneath your rough stepping beat.
The same son who split
his sister's head open with a spade
gave birds a Christian burial.

You always meant havoc to machines
taking them apart and leaving them in pieces
then skipping away
with their secrets in your pocket.

I tried to protect your golden joy
from a world waiting to steal your secrets,
and leave you in pieces,
a world greased with the blood
of young men like you.

Spend your gold, but keep your secrets
in your pocket, safe in the center
of your golden life, precious
as the last seed of an endangered species.
Let nothing steal your golden treasure.

Anniversary

Blossom by blossom our old love
unfolds new roses on an old bush
alive through fallow winters
and the harvest of passionate summers.

We prune away what has died
keeping what is alive of fifty-five years
together, nurturing and being nurtured
giving and receiving, more
than any singular reward
could give us a taste
sweet as the honey
from tropical wildflowers.

Growing older together we find room
for bright red adventures
encounters with butterfly fish
and the mysteries of New Zealand.

Surrendering to the intimacy
of an ancient rosebush
gnarled and thorny with age,
yet still producing spectacular
red roses served with grace
and fragrance upon our table.

Dolphin Encounter

As vulnerable as a teenager
waiting for a first kiss,
I kneel in a pool of water
ready for the dolphin's
round beak to touch my cheek.

I open my arms and am astonished
when a fish with the eyes of a mother
heaves itself upon my shoulder
embracing me against its heart.

Not just a trick done for fish
there is no hesitation or holding back,
but a sincere giving and receiving
of unexpected intimacy.

I rub my hands along its firm skin
smooth as wet silk
its underbelly as soft and white
as a baby's bottom, my joy
is that of a child who has leaped
naked from a bath, dripping and free.

Embraced by total acceptance, I join
the cosmic dance of a creature
more than fish, more than human
in the swiftness of its unconditional affection.

Letting Go

On the knife edge of expectation,
I let go of my donkey-will, the blinders
which plowed long rows of despair
and with the parachute of faith
strapped to my back,
I fall free through open windows and doors,
into uncharted regions
without boundaries or limitations
into the still strong core
where the mirror lake of the mind
sifts the static chaff
from the kernel of the pure wheat.

As I fall, I rise
into a courtyard with a fountain
where a golden chalice tips
and wine flows on to my parched lips.
Through my dry throat,
I speak words unknown and free.

Out of the cocoon of sleep,
I break free of the web of mistakes
ensnaring my butterfly will.
I emerge each morning new,
with a spring green step,
silver as leaves with tender shoots.
the fresh tendrils of my desire
reach out to every new thing, as if it all
had just been created before the wide
innocent eyes of the child
born in me each new day.

The beacon within my mind
makes a full circle and I walk over
the sky blue edge of the infinite
with my hands open.

Smoke

Summer is burning
somewhere nearby
its smoke obscures our perspective
of the opposite shore
with the hot breath of charcoal
and the suffocation of fear.

I shut my door to the smoke
and open my mind to determine
fake from true
real from false
the worldly from the spiritual
the empress or the devil's play.

Newspaper editorials and cartoons
portraying politicians as dogs
growling at their opponents
each one becoming what they call the other
defending their lies with confusions
their mendacity fouled with obscurity.

I seek the clarity under the chaos
stretching for the promise beyond
by burning what is no longer alive
in my fireplace to make room
for the fresh air after a rain
the warm sun illuminating
the sky with a clear, blue horizon.

Second Birth

To have come through the birth channel
of life and be born again
your own person, a child no more
of any mother, father or God,
at last an ancient one,
companion to the eternal.

This is no easy passage,
but less painful than going it alone,
or staying inside near the fire,
beside the hearth of someone else s
conception of who and what you are.

The keys to the doors were never
out upon the table. They are hidden
deep in secret drawers, within the silence
behind the center of your heart.

Only you can know which passions
could push you out of the narrows
into the places that burn away
all that keeps you buried.

This place at the table of belonging
holds your name, and the mystery
of your identity, with clues
to the secret of your destiny.

Ripe with age, you come
into the grace of the ancients:
the facility of discernment,
the confidence of magic,
the compassion that heals,
the empathy beyond sympathy,
rich in the faces of love,
mysterious and grand,
wearing the crown of age,
the majesty of your second birth.

Thor Holmstrom

He came from Sweden to gauge the giant trees
of the Northwest and to open a grocery store,
but his heart's strength was sapped
lifting crates of pork and beans.

He was to me a heavy silence
a dying man in a dark room
with no thunder in him,
only sadness, second hand memories,
and faded photographs.

Then came weeping for never knowing him
until many years later in a quiet vigil
while mourning the dead body
of my ninety two year old mother
his spirit spoke into my inner ear.

He told me to remember to honor
and be grateful not only to my mother,
but also for my stepfather, Ted Lundell,
a Finnish immigrant who saw
a widow overwhelmed with the care
of a grocery store and two fatherless daughters
and decided to love and adopt us as his own.

His spirit spoke of his gratitude to the man
who had been the only father I ever knew,
although a mechanical engineer with no affinity
for a grocery store, nor patience with customers.
Ted had protected and provided well
for our family after Thor no longer could.

Waging Peace

After years of struggle,
I pause and breathe-in
the pure essence of the earth,
and make a singular decision
to live in peace, at last.

Up here is a mountain meadow
where what seems to be
black and white,
right or wrong
can be seen
from a wiser point of view.

From here, I see over
the cities of confusions,
and feel the rivers of forever
streaming through my veins.

Here battles small and large
can be brought around
a full circle of forgiveness
to an open plateau of equanimity.

Here I can scatter wildflowers seeds
and plant bristle-cone, pine trees
in the rubble and ashes of battlefields
where the ruins of war used to reign.

Wise Wound

How you might have lingered
in the haven of childhood
until the wound
severed you from your past,
the misconceptions of who
you where meant to be.

The someone unknown
and different than
you had ever imagined,
the foreign face that felt
the pain of being
separated from the familiar.

After the blood of rebirth
washed you out,
you were pushed closer
to your truer self
the one only you could find.
.
No longer contained
or imprisoned within someone
else's idea of your identity,
you discover the door
out of your childhood
into a wondrous world you
would never have known
if you had remained confined
in a dark familiar wound.

What They Miss On the Way to the Falls

Some go to the falls for the joy
of that one big achievement
they can announce to their neighbor
or picture upon a photograph.

What they miss in their rush to the falls are:
a whole meadow full of purple larkspur,
the acrid smell of skunk cabbage,
a river bed full of ferns,
a entire hillside of trillium.

The splash and excitement of the falls
can blind them to the pink pussy paws,
the chocolate lilies, and the rare
lady's slipper hidden in the grass.

The roar of the falls can deafen
them to the chatter of chipmunks
high in the cedar trees,
the low moan of an owl.

In their rush to get to the falls,
they pass over the exquisite rocket
of the magenta shooting star,
without even a backward glance.

Inside / Out

We have turned it all backwards
with our focus on exteriors
everything measured by appearance
reduced to its smallest
molecule of insignificance

It is from the inside
it all starts, from the spark
of a new idea, or the flame
of a singular intent.

We have emptied out our lives
by denying or ignoring
rich interiors of complexity
the soft interior furniture
of hope that could comfort us.

Whole chapters of inner experience
have been denied or ignored
by religion and science
obsessed by reduction and sin.

Our minds are inside the mind
of the universe, where we can surrender
our separation for the greater wealth
of a heritage to be found within.

Discarding the heavy coats
of suffering and sin, we leave behind
the religious relics of colder seasons
stepping into the warm summer
of our earth, vulnerable and free.

Touching the Archetypes

Come with me to the edge of time and space
to touch the path of the formless forms
to trace their trajectory, to feel the warmth
of the ghosts of the more real
to hear the voice that calls us out of our sleep
and to dance with the music that makes us wise.

We can feel the life in that place
where life creates itself, and the essence
of what matters intersects our centers.
At this boundary, we can sense the secrets
that arise from its deepest streams.

Let us take the journey of the fool
who begins as a child, wide-eyed and open
not knowing where to go, but willing to explore,
willing to risk the unknown, willing to leap
off of cliffs without knowing what lies below,
trusting we will be supported by a hundred hands.

We do not remain as children long,
soon we become wise in unworldly ways:
wise as poet, painter, philosopher and musician.

We become artisans, explorers of the boundaries
each one experiencing the elephant of the unknown,
with unfamiliar and familiar senses.
Each one touches part of the whole:
the poet listens to its voice,
the painter sees its light,
the musician hears its music,
the philosopher knows its secrets.

How wonderful to be touched by the unknown!

Merlin

Magician extraordinary, rider of the wind,
more than man, more than fairy,
in his magic, in his tradition.
He knows the sacred
is a circle, the center
of which is everywhere,
the circumference nowhere.

If he goes far enough,
he will come back
to where he begins,
so he is not afraid to step
outside the lines or go too far
from what is known.

Balancer between worlds
with one foot on the earth
and one hand in the heavens.
He walks through doors
to other dimensions and returns
with Camelots and kings
crafted according to his will.

Confidante of owls and oaks,
tree talker, herb healer,
white dragon rider,
pioneer of the mists and mysteries
of what humanity can be,
of what can be known
of the magic land between,
heaven and earth.

He brings the more real
into the illusion, using the curve
of time and space to weave
and warp his magic web.

He knows when he stands
in the center of the sacred circle
he is clear as a crystal sphere

Escaping the Dark Wood

When we are lost in the midst of life,
we must quiet ourselves and listen
to each tree in our dark forest
knowing each one is there for a reason,
feeling our way, from tree to tree,
reading the roughness or smoothness
of the bark, like a blind man
reading the Braille messages
he finds with the tips of his fingers.

Then we can begin to get glimpses
of what no longer belongs:
the lifeless baggage of another time,
to make sense of the senseless,
and the heavy crosses of societies'
edicts of guilt and suffering.

To enter our new day,
we break our hearts open
just enough to begin to glimpse
the light streaming toward us
from a better place, where a new life waits for us
smooth and clear as the polished lens
of a telescope focused upon the stars.

Somewhere ahead, there is a place
clear and blue as a mountain lake
where the sun reflects a wonder
we once knew as children, yet is wise
with the heart and vision of an elder.

A Larger Plan

Every Spring the run-off through the swamp
poured polluted water into the lake
until the beavers arrived
and offered a bold solution.

With sharp-toothed determination,
they felled alder, aspen and birch trees
along the creek into the marsh
building dams that filtered
run-off from the spring streams.

The park ranger was wise enough
to stand by and watch the destroyers
of the forest have their way with the trees,
letting these natural engineers
do what they knew needed to be done.

The summer after the dams
appeared in the forest
the lake managers were astonished
to discover the water of the lake
was clearer and cleaner
than it had ever been before,
a natural solution found
for a perennial problem.

Grandfather Hill

At 96 with no aspirations to be 100
he basks in the home
he built years ago on a city lane
backed by a forest and a creek.
He apologizes for his clutter of books,
letters and pictures,
proudly displaying his favorites:
the picture of his great grand daughter
and the P38 lightning plane he flew
over Italy during World War II.

Whatever he encountered, he met
with courageous resilience.
Once over the Alps, one engine
of his two engine plane flamed up,
he shut it down and waited
ready to parachute out into the unknown,
with one engine left, he limped and sputtered
his way back to a foreign base.

When his defective heart nearly sputtered and died
he faced down the dire diagnosis
with decisive action; he stopped smoking,
became a vegan, played tennis in the summer,
cross country skiing in the winter.

He prefers diplomacy to divorce, talking
to fighting, and peace to war,
unless he was forced to defend himself.
He enjoys the company of attractive women
and was privileged as a fighter pilot
to be sent to a rest camp on the Isle of Capri.
Once he invited a pretty Italian girl to a dance.
She went only when chaperoned by her mother.

He loves his wife Helen who died at seventy five
but misses most the company of his last old friend,
a woman who died two years before.
She was a retired English teacher who shared
his love of the poetry by Tennyson and Wordsworth.

Floating the River

The river has its own time
of quickening in Summer
when the current stirs under your inner tube
and you launch out into a slack stream
as languid as cups in their saucers
waiting to be served
moving upon the silent breath of the water
forever forward inevitable as birth.

When the river slackens to syrup,
there is time to linger near the shore
and become familiar to the sun soaked stones
to watch the bull snakes slither into the grass
and probe the granite and golden stones below,
smooth as a baby's skull or the arms of a drowned maiden.

In this slow stream you can lie back
letting the river take you
giving up the struggle to get ahead
or tie together in a synergy of rubber circles
trying one way to paddle and then another
shedding those that frustrate or ensnare
connecting to conserve strength.

When it is the river's time
we are in the rapids
each one testing his or her strength alone
against a washboard of rocks
midst a cacophony of water clapping against stones
the applause of a great audience
where your courage expands or contracts
in a whirligig of spins and turns

when the water bears down
it is easy to get stuck in the shallows
to scrap an elbow or shin against the rocks
to be swept blind and backwards into the shoals
or to concentrate upon the door in the river
where your courage flowers
and you are a cup of red tulips
swept on to your birth.

Compass Flower

An inner compass points to our shattered
broken pieces of pain,
down to the ground of our bodies,
down to the earth beneath our feet.

We pause and listen to what
is crushed and splintered,
the bits and pieces of ourselves,
we must gather to stop
the hemorrhaging of our wounds,
to cleanse the blood of stagnation
and discard the shards of shame
cutting us into little pieces.

We collect our lost members,
soothing the edges of our sorrows
filling in the empty places of our grief.

We open like lilies to the sun
with the inner senses of a truer order,
more compassionate and real
than the needles of science
or all the finite calculations
of technologies of despair.

We hold the broken, lost pieces
of ourselves against our hearts,
where they are embraced,
accepted and comforted,
surrendering our separateness,
to our sense of home.

Cauldron Magic

The lady moves over the face of the water.
With her touch, the lake becomes a cauldron
stirred by waves of energy
pulsating in a mid-September wind.

She is gracious in her giving, gathering
and holding the possibilities in her lap,
where the unknown is known, before
it is possible. Here imagination
imagines itself and there is no need
for human fuel to light its fire.

The lady offers a sword of power
to anyone strong enough to hold it,
anyone willing to cut through their weeds,
and whatever clutters the quest
for which they have been called.

She stirs the pot and keeps passions hot
and brews the liquor which can stir
our passions and dreams alive.

The lady fills our nets with power and pours
her current into our creative streams.
She is the blood in our veins
through which rivers of creativity run.

She is the pot of gold at the end
of the rainbow. An ocean of ideas
are held in her lap, all that is possible
to conceive a world full of love and peace.

Confronting the Fire

"You need to leave now!" yells
a hysterical woman pounding on my door
She points to the red flames
devouring the hillside above us.

Whether to stay or go?
What to take or leave?
What matters most?

I focus on the living things needing protection:
the grandson who need to be awakened
the cat who needs to be caught and confined
the goldfish swimming in their tank.

We accept the offers of help from strangers
to hose down the roof
to capture the cat in a carrier
to carry the goldfish tank out to the car.

I thank the wise neighbor who had only months before
cleared away truck loads of dry pine needles
from the hillside above us
as a precaution to prevent an even larger fire,
we watch a fireman connect his pumper truck
to a nearby water hydrant and see the red tide turn
to the ethereal smoke
filling the air with pink hope.

The night is windless when a stranger asks
can she help carry out valuables from the house.
I tell her that won't be necessary. The fire
is drowned in water, choked in steam.

What really mattered in the fire of the moment
was what was alive and needing protection
leaving the rest to fate or the flames.

Reassurance

for Maxwell

Uncoiling into freedom,
after struggling in the womb
a white serpentine umbilical cord
slides through my dream
while my grandchild is being born

a turtle upon an open hand
is presented to me as a sign
he will survive
as a free, independent soul,
connected to our family
with protection given
to his precious life
by a friendly universe

a response to our prayers
and to his intent to breathe free,
to be born blessed
bringing the promise of his life
into our expectant world

Being Enough

Even though you do not know it,
you are as valuable as the stars waiting
to appear when their light arrives
spreading a cloak of silver over the sky.

Your worth is not something you have to earn
by good behavior. No reward is given
for good deeds or notorious achievements
you need only recognize the divine presence
 of a peaceful grace, a quiet magnificence
somewhere within.

Someday you will see it looking
at you through the mirror of a clear stream
accepting you just as you are,
your own best friend
with no need for the approval of others
or of a special lover to tell you
who you truly are.

Then you will know yourself
as you were first created to be
without knowing how,
without knowing why, the majesty
of divinity will meet your own
and you will be filled with sun.

Grace

Nothing is stronger
than the circle of innocence
from which we came.

Those who are enclosed in its strength
are invulnerable, they need no defense.
They are a fountain of pure water,
an ocean under the sail,
an open field of sunflowers,
a city without walls,
a world without arms.

Their hands reach back
through the circle of roses and fire
to touch the seeds of love
from which they came.

All of us will return home
in time
to this circle of innocence
this cervix of creation.

It is the halo around the Christ
born again
in every infant
the sacred wheel of invulnerable strength
toward which we all can turn.

Letter to my Grandson

for Alex

You do not have to bow beneath
the world's heavy measuring rod
or bend below the cruel instrument
of other's idea of perfection.
Nor do you need to kneel
before the altar of the little gods
of someone else's limited
conception of who you are.

I remember how bold you were as a child.
How strangers wondered at your adult words.
How you wallowed in ocean streams.
running naked without any shame,
carrying hope like a candle to a dark world.

Now you ride a unicorn of imagination
caught and warped by stories of war
what is honorable for a man. You are meant
to be so much more, part unicorn
with tender ways and winged words
more whole and free than any conventional man.

Listen to the call of your mountain gifts
trying to awaken you to a majestic vision
much more than the little stories told by old men
who urge you to fight some ominous enemy,
or shame will defeat your dreams.
No such enemy exists.

You have no idea how much you are loved.
How much help you have to reach your destiny.
Your story is grander than you now imagine.
How you belong to the earth, to the air
as true as the osprey diving into a lake
 belongs to the water and the sky.

You are here to help create a world
unlike the old, with less war, fear and sorrow
and more of what we all need to be free.

The Rebirth of Liberty Lake

When Liberty Lake was the putrid eye of a fish
left on the beach to rot,
the common sever
of a hundred years of human neglect,
the lake lovers would not concede
her to the snakes
bullfrogs and bloodsuckers.

They saw the black unruly hair
that clogged the underground streams
and stilled the motion of propellers
the mud that advanced upon the water
the algae that bloomed upon the vacated beaches,
but they would not leave.

They found an antidote
and poured it into the wound
cut back the long, unruly hair
and opened the clogged veins
of the virgin underground streams.

All morning I watch the grebes
dip their whole bodies into the lake
and bob back up again.
I look upon the face of the lake
that the light dresses and undresses
in green silk, azure and silver sheen
an ever changing impressionist painting
and thank the lake lovers

who saw the mud
and would not turn away.

Learning to Float

for Aden

What I hope he remembers
is the feel of my hands
under his back, supporting him
and my words of advice
"Trust the water, lie back
and let the water hold
up your body, your head.

Let the water be a pillow
and trust you are supported
and so are free to look up
at the blue dome of the sky
letting the water be a comfort.

Remember even when
I am no longer here to back you up
you are a son of the universe,
as precious as the lilies in the fields
as special as each sparrow in the sky.

If you will trust in a heritage of faith
unseen hands will always be there
to hold you when you need them."

The Visitation

In the healing room, one who is sunk
in a sea of grief, anguish and sorrow
sees with inner sight Jesus
standing above us, shaking his head
somewhat amused and compassionate:

It is not as tragic as you imagine, he says
This end of your parent's lives. They after all
are here on only a temporary stay, one filled
with satisfaction, without need for you to protect
them from everything. They have managed
even tougher times, and though your mother
appears frail, she is able to manage.

Your father is now on a different level
in the liminal, between worlds
where he is protected and safe, no longer
hooked, as you are, to this physical world.

"How can I be more compassionate?", she asks
Turn your compassion upon yourself.
If you can see yourself with the same compassion
with which you try to see others,
then you can open to be more creative,
spontaneous, self-accepting and free.

Advice of an Ancient One

An old crone invites me to sit and have tea,
then spreads out a feast of possibilities
upon the holiday table of my imagination
counseling me about what really matters.

She cackles as she drops
images of abundance upon my table:
airline tickets to New Zealand,
the warmth of summer
in what could have been my winter.

"You need to walk away from what others
call success," she warns,""For what they offer
will be salt to your thirst, dry bread
to your hunger for true success."

"You need to be willing to be a fool
who trusts the universe, but is wise enough
to turn away from the foolish."

"What matters is giving to others
 the gifts you have been given,
 the waters of healing, words that ring awake
the hearts of those who mourn."

"What matters most is touching
the place of eternity within you
where there is the peace and safety
of no beginning nor no end."

The Skin of the Earth

Who will speak for the trees
when their message
of strength
and peace is silenced?

Who will hold
us secure to the earth
when these great grandmothers
and grandfathers of the forest
have fallen into dust?

These ancient sentinels of strength
are sisters to the stars
inspiring us to reach upward
across the bridge of our limitations.

They are the skin of the earth
who help us breathe in inspiration
from the fertile force that opens
over their highest branches
under their deepest roots.

What will comfort us
when they are not here
to touch us with the gentle shade
of their pungent silence?

My Sacred Self

Deep calls to deep
out of the depths of being.
The question of "Who am I?"
rolls once more into my inner ear.

Silence speaks to that place
within me where there are no limitations.
So holy is that sacred place
its light extends to the farthest star
in it is a calm deeper than the blind fish
at the bottom of the sea.

This place knows itself and extends
outward to everything I touch.
Its strength is the pine tree
deeply rooted in stone.

Its devotion is the brown eyes of the dog,
its freedom as graceful
as swallows swooping low over the lake
it sings in the delicate throats
of the irises growing by the door.

What is sacred in me rises
like a tropical island hidden
under the surface of the sea
lush with coral gardens and seaweed beds
with white pearls of wisdom
already there upon its shore.

Surrender

Here on the shore of Liberty Lake
where the black lotus and lilac trees
whisper my name, I let in the oneness
the feeling of being home.

When the light of sunset transforms
the green water of the lake into gold,
I surrender my sense of separation
and am satisfied and fulfilled
in the late afternoon of my mind.

I am grateful this place found me
when I was in the dark woods,
lost and wandering down
from the cold dark days of Alaska
still looking for a home.

This place whispers, "Feel Free. Be at ease.
Enjoy yourself for an hour,
a day, a century. People dance
on this shore. You can too."

Here people smile and wave
and remember my name.
Here I can merge with blue shadows,
the green hills and Ponderosa pines
reflected in the ever changing luminous lake.
Here I can slip between time and space.
surrendering the spell of struggle.

Liberty

There is no shadow of turning
in the eye of the osprey
when the truth of what he seeks
becomes one with him
when he dives
plummeting beak
and brown feathers plunging after
down the sky.

Then the silver truth he seeks
quivers there within his talons
alive and dripping
above the surface of the lake
what was always there beyond
common sight is caught and held
up against the sky.

Dawn hits the sky
with a burst of blue light
scattering bright stars across the lake
and in the shadow of the houses
the sleepers awaken
one by one.

What each one looks upon
he or she becomes.
Some choose to be
a clear blue lake filled with stars
with clear blue minds

who see the morning stars
scatter their light across the lake
and grasp the blue wind beyond their fingertips.

The Giving Tree

The plum tree in our front yard
has been held together for years
by nylon tie downs, least it split
and fall upon the ground
yet every fall it bears
more and more plums.

Scarred and injured by storms,
it bears more than enough
to feed our family, the neighbors,
deer, raccoons and other night raiders.

Even when most of its bark
has been stripped from its trunk
by confrontations with cars,
insects and frosty weather
it keeps on giving.
No tree is more abundant
in its harvest. Its purple globules
grace our open hands
filling our hungry mouths
with sweet satisfaction.

Arrested Rivers

Once you could hear the rivers splash
and rage against these shores.
Now they lie stagnate and silent
held hostage by dams of concrete,
Bright salmon no longer leap up the falls
nor swim into the upper creative streams.

The dams have killed what was spontaneous and free.
The fish of tomorrow's feast are contained
within the clogged arteries and veins
of an imagination of scarcity,
a politics of oppression.

What becomes of the fish and the fishermen
is determined by men behind closed doors
who restrict what can or cannot spill
over the dams of defeat
through the turbines of destruction.

The stagnate rivers no longer feed the natives
nor the people who lived in harmony
with the relentless surge of the salmon
fighting to fulfill their heritage,
the freedom of their way home.

Nautilus

I cradle the abandoned home
of a deep sea mollusk in my hand
a chambered nautilus shell

split open to reveal
symmetrical float chambers
lined with mother-of-pearl
a lustrous underbelly of soft green
pink and violet luminescence

its spiral design has a symmetry
mysterious as the tides
powerful enough to float a submarine
or turn the wheels of a great machine
beautiful enough to spark
the movement of an ancient clock

when it lived, this mollusk transcended time
by creating this spiraling shell
and living in its newest chamber
it transcended itself
by emptying out past homes
so it could float away lighter
more open to possibilities
from a freer perspective

I am amazed by the hidden mysteries
of this model of transcendence
the luminous dimensions
of its miraculous powers

Wild Iris

Here in this meadow of myself
I seek the wild iris in me
the harmony of earth and water
to balance my fire and air.

I bury the bulb of my being
deep within my earth
some where inside me
a triangle of truth rises
too fragile for summer heat
blooming in a shady corner
of a pond of peace
where the slender dancers sway
their delicate petals rise
in a flame of silent prayer.

Their peaceful presence is accessible
when ever I pause to listen
with a passion to enter
beyond fragile filaments
to explore the sweet mystery
hidden beneath their royal purple
serpentine tongues
in a space sacred
as a thousand petaled lotus.

Getting out of the Way

so what is alive and true in me
can rest in my body
allowing me to be open
to the miracles of each moment
the surprises which go beyond
expectations or imagination

courage to step into the stream
letting go of the heavy furniture
of limiting beliefs no longer serving me
and the broken crockery
of dead relationships whose judgments
or opinions of my worth
are empty handed or hollow

I trust the stream flowing through me
favors and nurtures my longings
the direction given me by my birth name
Holmstrom, a home in a stream
marking my soul's desire
to move beyond dried up river beds
of constriction or inhibition

wisdom to know what can transform
times of confusion and chaos
bringing me extraordinary friends
I did not expect to meet,
sisters of the spirit, white sands in the desert,
lovers of the redwood forests,

poems expressing the rapture enfolded
in the deepest crevices of my mind

Celebration of a Storm

Dark clouds amass and spiral upward
in a hot summer sky.
There is a slow stirring of the wind
and the great trees shiver.
The waves clap an incessant beat against the shore
and within the house I hear
doors of the houses slamming shut
rain pelting the hot sidewalks.

Behind doors and windows
people wait for what is heavy and held
to be born. The sweet smell of wet earth
rises like steam from a volcano vent.

Then a silver vein strikes the dark sky.
The lake is illuminated with a lightning
so intense, its image remains
an afterbirth, an umbilical cord
silvered upon the retina.

Again and again
electric rivers chains and veins
expose the lake
and the silhouettes of trees
battered and wild
whipped and frenzied by the wind.

Behind their windows
those who belong to the storm
dance along the luminous currents,
They resonate to the rumble
of giant barrels rolling down the hills.
Silvered volts
scintillate through their veins
and along their nerves.
An ancient excitement
is born into their expectant world.

Meditation

Let us
fall into the lap
of the valley of love

Let us
lift
as mist lifts
over a cold lake
on a late September morning

Let us
leave behind:
the world of one and two,
the world of rush and go,
the world of right and wrong,
the leaves of our past lives

Let us
fall as water falls
over rock ledges
where even the plants listening
for the light

Let us enter the world of the inner ear
where the light waits
for us to hear its music

The Goddess of Democracy

Although there is no monument now to her in Tienanmen Square,
she still stands white and flaming
within the minds of those who remember her sweet promise,
the power of her upraised hand that holds
the greatest gift of all, the torch of choice
always there to be taken by those who will not live
without the light of her freedom.

Crying for their freedom, the young Chinese students
placed all their aspirations into her construction
the clear-eyed dreamers who dared to raise
her bold white body against the hard stones
of their father's square.

That night she came down in crumbled pieces of plaster
among the shock of gunfire and young bleeding bodies
her power plundered, the highest price paid
by dreamers hunted down by uniformed officials
what she gives freely oppressed, persecuted, denied
but never conquered.

She is the pure freedom
we remember before our birth
the promise never to be denied
the sweet celebration of choice
held up for those who would grasp
its hope and pass it on to those forerunners
out in front bearing the torch
of her burning and ever growing desire.

The Insurrection

"We will never give up. We will never concede,"
the president told his supporters inciting them
to be strong to move toward the Capitol
to fight for the election stolen from him.

With his encouragement, the mob of rioters
climbed up the stone stairs and balconies
swarming like hornets over the barriers,
wild beasts with buffalo horns and red hats
smashing in doors with axes and metal pipes
breaking windows, entering the hallowed halls
private offices and restricted places
violating the sanctity of a sacred place

The mob desecrated the chambers of the Senate,
smashing through the doors to the House of Representatives
stealing computers and making mayhem with public property,
assaulting police and news reporters in an angry attempt
to prevent congress from certifying a new president
who by all legal measures had won a fair election

After the siege on the Capitol was over, he addressed
his supporters asking them to go home in peace
saying he loved them and considered them special,
making no apologies for encouraging them to desecrate
the Sacred Temple of Democracy, he had once sworn
an oath to preserve, protect and defend.

Going Home

So poignant is my passion to go home
 it draws me ever closer
to the center of creation,
as surely as the magnet of the North
pulls the geese out of the South.

Beyond the snarl of childhood nets,
I climb our the cradle of my consciousness,
throwing off the weight
of heavy blankets of fear.

So strong is my passion to go home,
I listen to those who promise to show
me the way. I buy a ticket on their bus
and am taken for a ride, only to be dumped
on a strange corner, with a laugh.

I grow wiser, remembering the promise
of the rainbow sewn into all my cells,
If I walk out into the water,
 I can trust myself to swim.

If I climb the mountain
I will enter the light that shines
at the summit of awareness
and feel the rainbow's rain
falling golden upon my hair.

Credits and Publication Information

George Sabo of Nome Alaska in 1994 created and performed music and actress, Pamela Thomas read for a taped production of eighteen of Eleanor Limmer's poems called "The Skin of the Earth." This tape included the poems "Celebration of a Storm," "The Skin of the Earth," "Meditation," and "Letting Go." and "Liberty."

"Celebration of a Storm" and "Liberty" appeared in a collection of Inland Northwest Poets called **Deep Down Things** edited by Ron McFarland, Franz Schneider and Kornel Skovajsa published by The Washington State University Press of Pullman Washington in 1990.

"The Skin of the Earth" was included in the book PoetryAlaskawomen-Top of the World edited by Professor Suzanne Summerville, Arts Venture, Fairbanks Alaska, 1993.

"Floating the River" and "Healing the Child Within" appeared in a collection of four Alaskan women poets entitled **Whispered Secrets** published by Sedna Press in 1991.

Poems from **An Alchemy of Joy** published by Freedom Press in 2000 reprinted by the permission of the author and publisher are these: "Bushwhacking" " Storm Water-Runoff" "Returning Home" "Arrested Rivers" "Connections" "My Sacred Self"
"Going Home" "Meditation" "Letting Go" "The Goddess of Democracy" and "Liberty." "Rebirth of Liberty Lake."

William Berry a composer and musician with the Spokane and Walla Walla Symphony has written the music for the lyrics of the poem "Merlin" part of a musical he and Eleanor Limmer created together called **Return of the Great Round** in 2005 Max Mendez sang this tribute to Merlin in the role of Arthur.

"The Rebirth of Liberty Lake" appeared in **An Alchemy of Joy in 2000 and The Restoring Liberty Report** written in 1989 on the restoration of Liberty Lake.